Through My Eyes

RYAN KASPER

Through My Eyes

Copyright © 2024 by Ryan Kasper.

MILTON & HUGO L.L.C.
4407 Park Ave., Suite 5
Union City, NJ 07087, USA

Website: *www. miltonandhugo.com*
Hotline: *1- 888-778-0033*
Email: *info@miltonandhugo.com*

Ordering Information:
Quantity sales. Special discounts are granted to corporations, associations, and other organizations. For more information on these discounts, please reach out to the publisher using the contact information provided above.

Library of Congress Control Number: IN-PROCESS
ISBN-13:   979-8-89285-136-7   [Paperback Edition]
                979-8-89285-137-4   [Hardback Edition]
                979-8-89285-138-1   [Digital Edition]

Rev. date: 05/01/2024

DEDICATIONS

To God, and my family.
To Karla Maria Cortes for courage
To Sarah DiGaetano for push,
And Garrett Stumbaugh, for resilience.

Special Thanks to Daniel Fitzgerald who showed me who a leader ought to be.

Thank you to everyone who has played a part in my life thus far. And special dedication to the 11th, 46th, and 15th Engineer Battalions and my larger Army family.

Always with Love
-Ryan Kasper

Before you read- Everything contained within these pages are a result of thoughts and emotions I have had about the world, through my perspective, with my creative lens. No piece is a summary of any actual event that occurred, but instead emotions from similar situations and characters may allude to feelings that real people have made me feel, however no person mentioned or alluded to is real. But instead reflections of real people and perceptions combined together within my mind and from my heart. If we are crafting a being of emotion, let my words be the bones, and your thoughts can be the flesh. Let's begin,

SUNRISE

Once there was nothing, then all at once nothing sprang forth into everything, and in the chaos, stars were born. One such star had several planets, but on one particular planet, something peculiar happened. A small part of existence woke up. Prior to its waking up, it was no different from the universe around it, all the same building blocks, all the same rules. However, just put together in the perfectly perfect way so as to bend the rules around it, it wouldn't happen all at once, and it would take time, lots of it. But over time, this small piece of existence that had woken up—life— became more and more complicated. Until one day, there was man.

The tiny piece of existence that had woken up asked a simple yet profound question. "Why?" This question, while so simple, was next to impossible to answer. The very concept of it, to know what why means, there is no physical item bound to the word, there is nothing you can show someone to explain what the question "why" means, but all the same, we all know the word's meaning. In the same way, you cannot meaningfully describe a color to a blind person, you cannot describe the question of why to someone who doesn't understand it. But that's the thing is we all inherently understand it.

Through space and time, the violent explosions and collisions of atoms formed stardust, it formed the elements. The elements arranged into the shape of us. Into the shape of me. Every living being that I'm descended from has their story, all the way back to the beginning and they have passed on the torch to the next generation time and time again, to continue to attempt to perfect life itself. So the weight of a thousand generations, and the untold secrets of the universe, the secrets of me, as I am part of the universe, meaning the universe is me and I am the universe, as is everyone. The question "why" has become my responsibility. Yet like all of those who came before, I do not know the answer.

I know what it is like to be a child, to feel the sun on my skin and the grass on my feet as I run through the yard, I know the feeling of my mother's hug after I scraped my knee. I know the pride on my father's face after I hit a baseball. The tears in his eyes as I graduate basic training, my mother running to hug me after a year apart. My brother and I understanding each other in a way no one else could understand us. I also remember the simple things like the warmth of another hand in yours, or the slight shifting of weight as someone leans into you, or the feel of a hand behind your head as you're pulled into a kiss. The feeling of betrayal, the feeling of disbelief when you thought you could count on someone, the feeling if you could just make them understand how bad they hurt you then they'd care. The feeling when you realize that they do know, they just don't care. They just don't. For every experience, for every thought, every feeling, an untold number of lifetimes precede it. My ancestors' lives flowing through me in my own and specific unique way. Within all of this, I cannot ascertain the meaning of life, if there truly is one or not, and with all the highs and lows and meaningful moments lost to the ages, it brings me no closer to the question of "why? What's the point?".

RYAN KASPER

Allow me to tell you where it leads. It's 30,000 years in the future, I have just woken up from cryosleep. After being frozen for 30,000 years, I step onto the ground of this alien world. It feels like home. But the smell of the place is something I've never smelled before. I walk up the ridge to the ocean and overlook the waves, filled with glowing plankton and creating an ethereal effect. I look up to the rising dual stars and think of my father. 30,000 years has he been gone. 30,000 years since I've seen that look of pride on his face, 30,000 years ago my mother held her crying baby in her arms. And I continue to look out to the rising sun, far from home and among the stars, through all of the generations that lead to me. I see my father's smile in the sky. In the universe's eyes, I can see his pride. Maybe one day we'll know why. But until then I am the custodian of my heart, and I shall take care of the question "why?" Because I am the mystery. I am the question.

Always with Love,
Ryan

VOID

To contemplate my place in the vast horizon's span,
I ponder who I am, what I am, and the grand plan.
The age-old question, "Where did we originate?"
Rattles my mind, a mystery so intricate and great.
I am the mystery, the atoms and the matter,
Weaved into awareness, a cosmic chitter-chatter.
Built a vessel to interact, to touch and to dream,
To imagine, to alter the flow of the cosmic stream.
A part of the universe that realized its own face,
Decided to change, to join the universal embrace.
I am an enigma, the question of how and why,
Powerful indeed, under the vast, endless sky.
Awareness isolated by experiences of its own,
Reaching out, seeing others, yet feeling alone.
For we can't see through each other's eyes, feel each other's heart,
In this dance of existence, together yet apart.
Each word, every glance, an attempt to bridge the divide,
To connect, to express, in this journey we ride.
Yet isolated we remain, in our minds, we reside,
Wondering why, in our silent, internal guide.

RYAN KASPER

Perhaps we don't need to know why, to embrace the dance,
Maybe it's enough, two awarenesses' chance,
To understand each other, under the sun's vast expanse,
Not knowing who or why, but giving the sunrise a glance.
Despite the sun's rise, for eons before and beyond our breath,
Its endurance through time, a testament to life and death.
The questions of who and why, as we take our earthly step,
Fade in the beauty of the moment, our shared depth.
A momentary blip, maybe, but ours to keep,
In the beauty of the sunrise, a memory to seep.
Two awarenesses together, in the vastness, so steep,
Enjoying the sunrise, in our hearts, to forever leap.

Always with Love,
Ryan

SLOW BURN

I have gazed upon the vast expanse of universes, looked deeply, and then turned away, grateful for the life I have been given.

Yet, sometimes, when I lift my eyes to the stars, I feel a slow burn igniting within my soul. It's the ache of "what if things had gone differently?" The sting of enduring someone's cold apathy cuts deep. To love profoundly, to care without measure, only to be met with indifference and avoidance is a unique torment.

In moments of despair, I find myself lashing out against the universe itself, my outcry serving both as a plea and a prayer to the divine. I beg for mercy, for a shift in fate's cruel flow, for the winds of change to blow in my favor. My heart screams for what it yearns, shedding all denial to confess, "This is what I desire, even if it brings me shame."

My anger, rage, and pain converge into a singular point of focus. With such intensity, I wish to ignite an ember so fierce it pierces through reality itself, compelling the cosmos to acknowledge my suffering, to invoke divine compassion to act on my behalf.

RYAN KASPER

I envision myself falling to my knees, acknowledging my limitations, admitting I lack the power to alter the immutable. In surrender, I shed the facade of strength, strip away the ego, arrogance, and every defense I've meticulously constructed. To stand, soul bared, devoid of pretense, vulnerable and unequivocally genuine, is to invite salvation from circumstances beyond my redemption.

Until that moment of grace, my soul endures this slow burn—a hidden, persistent pain, awaiting the day it might finally heal into a scar.

Always with Love,
Ryan

REFLECTIONS

In the quiet, I lay on my bed, wrapped in a stillness only I can know. My gaze was fixed on the ceiling, but my mind roamed far beyond the confines of this room, wandering through the corridors of what-if. In this introspective trance, I experienced something supernatural and extraordinary: I began to see glimpses of the countless lives I might have led in other universes.

One universe revealed a dazzling alternate reality where I was a football legend. I was the star running back, basking in the glory of a Super Bowl victory. The cheers of the crowd as they chanted my name, the weight of the trophy in my hands, and the adoration in the eyes of fans – it was a life of fame and athletic triumph, so far removed from the routine of my life.

In another universe, I found myself in a quaint, sunlit café, across from her, the girl who had once captured my heart. In this world, we had never parted; our love had grown and flourished. I watched as we laughed together, our hands entwined, surrounded by a life built on shared dreams and enduring love.

I saw more: a universe where I was a celebrated author, my words touching the hearts of millions; another where I was a groundbreaking entrepreneur, shaping the future with my vision; and yet another where I found fulfillment in teaching, my days filled with the joy of nurturing young minds.

But the flow of universes was not woven with joy alone. In one heart-wrenching scene, I was struggling with addiction, lost and alone, a stark contrast to the hero on the football field. Another showed me as an orphan, my childhood marked by loneliness and longing. There was even a universe where I had never left my small hometown, trapped in a life of unfulfilled potential, haunted by the ghost of what could have been.

As I witnessed these lives – each a reflection of different choices, different chances taken or missed – I felt an overwhelming mix of emotions. There was wonder and longing for the heights I reached in some lives, and a profound sadness for the depths of despair I encountered in others.

It was my truest friend, who brought me back to my reality. "Ryan, you up for some ice cream?" she asked, her voice a lifeline back to the present.

Walking to the ice cream shop, the normalcy of the act was grounding. The laughter, the mundane decisions over flavors, the simple pleasure of the moment – it all felt precious, a stark reminder of the beauty in the everyday.

My phone vibrated with a message from my dad, "Mom and I love you very much!" It was a simple, powerful affirmation of the love that anchored me in this universe, in this life.

In that moment, I realized the profound beauty of my own journey. Each universe had its own joys and sorrows, but this life – my life – was unique in its combination of experiences, relationships, and choices. Embracing my reality, with all its imperfections and possibilities, I found a new appreciation for my path, determined to live fully in the world that was uniquely mine. "And I think might just be enough." I thought.

Always with Love,
Ryan

RYAN KASPER

SUN AND MOON

Once upon a time, in a world not unlike our own, there thrived a friendship so subtle yet profound that its story, though largely lost to the sands of time, continues to echo through the ages. Their names have been forgotten, and the span of their camaraderie remains hidden in the mists of history, but the legacy of what they shared is immortal. He was a being of curious temperament, a seeker of truth and wisdom, and she, a vibrant soul, thirsty for knowledge that the cosmos held within its vast embrace.

Their paths crossed at a serendipitous moment, perhaps orchestrated by the stars themselves, initiating a bond that transcended mere friendship. He, with years lending him wisdom, became her mentor, her guiding northern star, illuminating her journey towards realms of understanding. In him, she found not just a teacher, but a kindred spirit, a true companion in the quest for life's deeper meanings. They explored mysteries and marveled at the universe, side by side, their spirits forever enriched by reciprocal respect and admiration.

Yet, as is the way of all mortal beings, a day came when the ephemeral nature of life summoned them to part from the physical world. Their bodies surrendered to the inevitable destiny, but their essences, resilient and eternal, refused to yield to the void. In the afterlife, they emerged anew, not as flesh, but magnificent, resplendent energy.

Reunited in this ethereal dominion, they danced, swirling and twirling with a freedom unknown to their earthly forms, radiant spectra trailing behind them in joyous celebration of their unbreakable bond. As they wove through the stars, their conversation, light as cosmic dust, turned to a shared aspiration, a new purpose for their undying alliance.

In a decision sparked by altruistic unity, they chose to become everlasting celestial guardians, the twin spirits of the sun and moon. He embraced the sun, a bold, nurturing force, spreading hope and vitality with his golden rays, banishing darkness at every dawn. She adopted the moon, a serene, ethereal beacon, using her silvery light to protect the night, guiding dreamers and travelers alike.

Though destined to exist in an eternal dichotomy, governing the skies at opposing intervals, they found solace in their shared purpose and the brief, precious moments of their meeting at dawn and dusk. In these quiet, shimmering minutes, the world caught glimpses of their affection for one another, painting the sky with hues of their tender reunion.

Together yet apart, they continue their vigilant watch, the guardians of diurnal light and nocturnal brilliance. Their story, silent but for the whispers that ride the dawn, serves as a testament to friendship's undying resonance, a celestial symphony played out in the infinite theatre of the universe. And so, even as they light up the world from their distant realms, their tale lives on, a human memory cradled in the heart of the cosmos.

Always with Love,
Ryan

DREAM ON

A storm within, a raging torrent, emotions' wild dance,
I struggle, I fight, I pull myself to take my stance.
Commanding the sea, I rise, I ascend,
I am the master, the captain, this voyage won't end.
A burning chaos, a dance in darkness' hold,
Smoldering, churning, a mystery to unfold.
Yet, I dream to pull beauty from this tempest's might,
To weave wonder from chaos, to create a dazzling light.
I seek not to be consumed, but to form something divine,
To pull the radiant from the shadow, to make the hurricane benign.
To craft something beautiful amid turmoil's wild wave,
Something that catches the eye, a soul to save.
Not to enrapture or capture, to make others bow or heed,
But to inspire them to think, to plant a creative seed.
"What can I weave? What can I make?" Let them muse,
In that moment, our souls touch, an ethereal fuse.
To truly see and be seen, I must bare it all,
The angel and the devil, every rise and fall.
The anger, pain, shame, regret – all parts of me,
A complex puzzle, the essence of humanity.

How can one soul unveil what's pure and true,
Expose something raw, beautiful, and then undo?
A love so profound, willing to give all and more,
Only to turn to ash, leaving wounds to the core.
The truest tragedy, not a crime born of evil's seed,
But a crime of apathy, a careless, callous deed.
No purpose in the pain, no reason or cause,
Just a void left behind, a soul with gaping flaws.
Dream on, for the storm continues to roar,
The voyage persists, new horizons to explore.
In the chaos, the beauty, the love and the loss,
I find my strength, my passion, at whatever cost.
For I am the master, the weaver of dreams,
I am the light that pulls from chaos and gleams.
Through connections, emotions, the human I want to be,
I continue to dream, to create, to truly be me.
In the crucible of existence, where emotions wildly clash,
A vision emerges, clear and bright, from the relentless thrash.
A desire not just to endure, but to transcend the gloom,
To pull from the chaos a radiant bloom.

How long and malevolent the journey seems,
A path laden with shattered dreams.
Yet a crime not of malice, but of simple disregard,
A wound left open, unhealed, and scarred.
But should it be a crime of hatred, at least it's aimed at me,
At least the pain has purpose, a reason I can see.
But this agony is aimless, born of apathy's cold embrace,
A torment without cause, a never-ending chase.
What strength lies in connection, a touch so pure and deep,
To find within another a love you wish to keep.
A bond that seems eternal, willing to give it all,
Only to crumble into nothing, a deafening silent call.
How can the same hand that once unveiled a love so divine,
Turn it into ashes, break this heart of mine?
A tragedy unfolds, not in evil's twisted grin,
But in indifference's gaze, where nothingness begins.
Yet I dream on, for I am more than what was done to me,
I'm a tempest, a creator, a boundless, raging sea.
I will weave my thoughts into something wild and true,
A collage of existence, a world that's ever new.
In the pain and the beauty, the love and the loss,
I find my essence, my soul's embossed.

RYAN KASPER

I am the master, the weaver of my fate,

I am the dreamer who dreams, it's never too late.

For beneath the surface of all that seems real,

Lies a power, a passion, a longing to feel.

To touch the fabric of the universe and find,

A connection, a vision, a love undefined.

So dream on, for the voyage is far from its end,

The storm continues, and new paths will ascend.

Through the chaos, the wonder, the human embrace,

I continue to dream, to love, to chase.

For I am the master of my sea, the captain of my soul,

I am the dreamer who dreams, and in dreaming, I am whole.

Rage, rage, rage, so much anger, frustration, pain,

A tempest unleashed, a wild, uncontrolled refrain.

A fury born of wounds, of loss and betrayal's sting,

A fire that burns, an unending, tormenting ring.

Within this chaos, a question begins to rise,

Why this anger? Why these tears in my eyes?

Is it the hurt from the past, the wounds left unhealed,

Or a longing for something more, a truth yet revealed?

I search for answers in the storm's relentless churn,

In the fire's wild dance, I seek, I yearn.

For beyond the anger, the frustration and despair,
Lies a calling, a purpose, something rare and fair.
To touch history's fabric, to grasp the human plight,
To break free from the trap, to take my own flight.
The conflict rages, a battle within my core,
To follow the path laid, or to seek something more?
Should I conform, accept the status quo's embrace,
Or reach out, disturb the current, find my own space?
To look past illusion, past structures and concepts defined,
To shape my world, live and die, truly unconfined.
Am I wrong to desire, to want to leave my mark?
To be more than a number, to ignite a creative spark?
To step out of the shadows, to challenge, to dare,
To look underneath the underneath, to truly care.
In the eyes, I find understanding, a shared dream,
A glimpse of something more, a world yet unseen.
For in our chaotic existence, rigid with strife and turmoil,
Lies a plan, a golden seam, a reward for our toil.
Broken things can be mended, cracks filled with gold,
A reminder that we're more than the roles we've been told.
We set out to find ourselves, to dive deep within,
Only to discover our mind anchored with another's kin.

So dream on, dream on, for the journey's not done,
Through rage and longing, our true selves are won.
In the storm, the wonder, the connection so divine,
We continue to dream, to create, to intertwine.
To find myself in a million pieces, scattered, torn,
To gaze upon the fragments of a being forlorn.
In the darkness they lie, yet within them I find,
A glimmer of hope, a golden spark, a sign.
With hands trembling, yet with purpose and might,
I weave the darkness into a fabric of golden light.
I pull it all together, every shard, every trace,
I will them to rise, to assemble, to take their place.
They rise and arrange in beautiful array,
A testament to strength, to grace, a new way.
To be the new me, golden, beautiful, and free,
To cut through life, to be everything I want to be.
No longer confined by the pains of the past,
No longer bound by shadows that were cast.
I step into the light, radiant and whole,
A being reborn, with a clear and focused goal.
I am the weaver of my destiny, the dreamer of my dream,
I am the artist of my life, and nothing's as it seems.

For beneath the surface of turmoil and strife,

Lies the power to create, to breathe new life.

In the chaos and wonder, in love's embrace,

I find my true self, my purpose, my place.

I am the master, the captain, the guiding star,

I am the dreamer who dreams, no matter how far.

So dream on, dream on, let your soul take flight,

Embrace the storm, the darkness, and find your light.

For you are more than the sum of your parts,

You are a universe unto yourself, a work of art.

In every tear, in every laugh, in every silent plea,

Lies the potential to be golden, beautiful, and free.

So weave your fabric, let your shards rise and shine,

For you are the dreamer, and the dream is thine.

Always with Love,

Ryan

SMILE AGAINST THE FEAR

Upon a ship, so wild and free,
In storms that dance on raging sea,
I sit atop the swelling sail,
Where thunder roars and winds assail.
I look into her eyes, concern they hold,
A fear of storms, untamed and bold,
But as I laugh, I see her smile replace the fear,
And laughter overtakes her too, my dear.
With laughter ringing through the night,
Defying storms with pure delight,
A joyful dance with wind and rain,
Embracing chaos, feeling no pain.
The lightning flashes, a frenzied dance,
Yet in our eyes, a tranquil glance,
A knowing smile, a peaceful gleam,
At one with nature's wildest dream.
With hands stretched wide to touch the sky,
Souls so free, prepared to fly,
In laughter's song and thunder's plea,
And then we were all happy and free.

Always with Love,
Ryan

SKY WITHIN

Beneath the Sakura tree, kneel, surrender, just be,
Feel the breath within, the wind without, in life's symphony.
Exhale your essence into the wild, vast world,
Inhale its strength, in your heart unfurled.
Breathe without, sky within, the mantra begins.
Children of information, we command answers at our fingertips,
Yet the wisdom to ask has embarked on an eclipse.
The eager flame of learning, crushed under greed's oppressive shoe,
Within the depths of me, I seek the answers that are true.
Questions echo, reverberating in the labyrinth of my mind,
In the ocean of information, shouldn't answers be kind?
I am unique, I am the only version of me,
A mystery decoded solely by my key.
An awareness bestowed in skin, bone, and human clay,
Charged with the Earth's journey, a cosmic play.
But for what grand purpose? For why, under the infinite sky?
In this world crafted by the countless, is it wrong to wish to be
seen?
To yearn to etch my existence, to touch history's sheen?
A longing to leave an indelible mark, my footprints in the sand
of time,
Yet constrained by the chain of human paradigm.

RYAN KASPER

All seem to flow in the direction preordained, maintaining the sequence,

The incessant march towards conformity, the relentless insistence.

Yet can't I stir the current, challenge the consequence?

Reach out, disrupt the pattern, shatter the pretense?

To step beyond the towering cityscapes, the rigid structures, the confined lines,

To sculpt my world, carve my destiny, assert my signs.

A tug-of-war, the pull of tradition versus the call of the untamed,

A yearning to be part of the dance, yet to dance unrestrained.

The urge to break free, to escape the cage,

Yet to touch the fabric of the world's stage.

Is it a futile dream, in this quest that is mine,

To hope another soul would dare to intertwine?

To peer beneath the beneath, unravel the illusion's design?

Amid the clamor of the universe, space and time,

A lone voice cries out, "Behold me!" echoing in the divine.

Then, and only then, shall our visions align, she will perceive me.

She will discern that she is her, he'll recognize he is him,

In our turbulent world, edging on the precipice's brim.

Yet, I firmly believe, a plan subtly unfurls, under the chaos's whirl,

Behind the fractures, a gleaming promise of gold, a life-affirming pearl.

A reminder that broken shards can be mended, rebound,
In the exploration of ourselves, a common resonance is found.
We might embark to discover our depths, voyaging the open sea,
Only to anchor our minds in a harmonious harbor, cradled in
another's decree.

Always with Love,
Ryan

THE QUIET MOMENTS.

In the space between
The hustle and bustle
Neither here nor there
Lay the quiet moments.
In those brief moments
It's as if the world pauses
And I am in a universe
Unto myself
Alone and cast adrift
In the current of my own mind.
Joys and sorrows
And everything in between.
In the calm of the between I am aware
But it gives rise to the storm of my thoughts.
And while the moments are bliss
And I hate to be pulled from them
If I am to be pulled out
I'm glad that it's you.

Always with Love,
Ryan

THE DRAGON AND THE FOX

Under an oak of magic, a friendship did shoot.
Lived a fox spirit, nimble and spry,
A playful glint always in her eye.
One day in the creek, she spied a sight,
A dragon, small, a mere sprite.
Not a baby, just a dragon small,
Lost in the world, he'd taken a fall.
"Oh, you're lost," she said with a playful tease,
On his prickled pride, she did lightly seize.
"I'm not lost!" he said with a goofy grin,
"Just can't find my home, don't know where to begin."
With a chuckle and nudge, she agreed to guide,
Through the mystical forest, side by side.
They ventured forth, through wood and stream,
Their growing bond, like a sunbeam.
To a towering mountain, their journey led,
"Is this your home?" to the dragon she said.
With a confident nod, he looked at the peak,
"Let's climb," she said, giving his paw a tweak.
Up the rocky face, they bravely climbed,
Their friendship deepened, beautifully timed.

RYAN KASPER

At the mountaintop, his home stood grand,
Yet empty it was, not as he'd planned.
But the fox, with a twinkle in her gaze,
Said, "You can stay with me, for the rest of your days."
Under the oak, they found respite,
In the heart of the forest, under the starlight.
That night a thunderstorm did roar,
As they curled up on the forest floor.
The tale of the fox and dragon's quest,
In the heart of the forest, forever at rest.
So here's to friendships, formed in delight,
In the magical forest, under the moonlight.
The dragon and the fox, a pair so odd,
Bound by a bond, deep and broad.
Their story of laughter, banter, and mirth,
Echoes in the forest, a tale of worth.
Proof that friendship can take any form,
And together, we can weather any storm

Always with Love,
Ryan

WARMTH

On a chilly evening, when the sky was cloaked in heavy clouds and the rain poured down in a relentless symphony against the earth, a lone traveler trudged through the wet wilderness. Each step was a splash, each breath a cloud in the crisp air, as the cold seeped through clothing and skin alike, chilling to the bone. Nature, in its vast, untamed beauty, had unleashed a storm that transformed the world into a canvas of grey and silver.

Finally, the weary traveler arrived at a quaint, secluded cottage, nestled at the edge of a whispering forest. The cottage, with its warm, inviting glow, stood as a beacon of comfort against the dreary backdrop of the rain-soaked landscape. Pushing the door open, the traveler was immediately enveloped in a cocoon of warmth.

Inside, a hearty fire crackled and popped in the stone fireplace, casting a lively dance of flames that illuminated the room with a soft, golden hue. The fire's warmth reached out like loving arms, chasing away the chill that had settled deep in the traveler's bones. The room was filled with the comforting sound of the fire's crackle and the faint patter of rain against the windows, a melody that spoke of safety and shelter.

The traveler shed the soaked coat, the heavy weight of the damp fabric a stark contrast to the light, warm air of the cottage. Approaching the fireplace, the heat greeted like an old friend, wrapping around in a gentle embrace. The flames, with their hypnotic flickering and warm colors ranging from deep oranges to vibrant reds, were a visual feast, a contrast to the grey world outside.

Settling into a cozy armchair by the fire, the traveler stretched out tired limbs, feeling the warmth seep into every pore, every chilled finger and toe beginning to tingle back to life. The heat caressed the skin, drying the dampness, loosening the tight muscles, and easing the cold-induced stiffness.

As the fire's warmth continued to work its magic, the traveler gazed into the flames, watching as they danced with a life of their own. The gentle crackling sound, the soft glow, and the comforting heat together weaved a spell of relaxation and peace. The chaos of the storm outside faded to a distant memory, overshadowed by the tranquility of the moment.

With each passing minute, the traveler's spirit was rejuvenated, the stress and fatigue melting away in the fire's embrace. The cottage, with its roaring fire, became a sanctuary, a haven from the storm, a place where warmth and comfort reigned supreme.

Outside, the storm raged on, but inside, there was only the blissful warmth, the soothing crackle of the fire, and a sense of serene contentment. The traveler, now warm and dry, closed their eyes, surrendering to the peacefulness of the moment, grateful for the refuge from the storm, in the heart of a warm, comforting fire.

Always with Love,
Ryan

TRIANGLE

In the quiet twilight, 'neath the cosmic dome,
Here we stand, a trio, yet each so alone,
Invisible chasms, though fingertips graze,
Uniting our silences, in intricate ways.
Lost thoughts echo in the vacuum vast,
Shadows of dreams, from the future, the past,
Million miles cross, in inches of space,
As we search the stars for a saving grace.
A triangle, equidistant, equilateral,
Straining the bonds, both fragile and lateral,
In our eyes, galaxies spiral in play,
Yet unsaid words keep us galaxies away.
Do we dare, to bridge the cosmic sea?
Hand over our thoughts, set the secrets free?
Or do we anchor them, in abyssal zone,
Where starlight's touch has never shone?
Between the silence, the speech, a fine seam,
Reality blurs into a distant dream.
A paradox, profound, in the celestial tone,
Together we stand, yet utterly alone.
In this geometric dance, we continue to sway,
The Triangle of existence, in persistent fray.
Through time we traverse, in sorrow or glee,
Forever apart, yet together, are we.

Always with Love,
Ryan

A CREATOR AND HIS CREATIONS

In a world of normalcy, surrounded yet isolated, a lonely wanderer sought answers to himself. This seeker, burdened by an unyielding solitude, turned inward, his spirit delving into the depths of his own being. In this profound introspection, he unearthed a radiant spark—a beacon that illuminated a path to divinity.

With each step on this ascendant journey, the seeker found himself dissolving into the fabric of time itself. He became a silent witness to epochs and eras long past: he watched in awe as Christ shouldered the weight of the cross; he observed the Romans as they laid the foundations of an empire destined to echo through history. His ethereal travels led him to the Great Library of Alexandria, where he absorbed wisdom penned by hands long turned to dust. He gazed upon the pyramids, those eternal sentinels of mankind's ingenuity and ambition.

Yet, in his timeless wanderings, a yearning grew within him—a desire to create, to forge something as enduring as the wonders he had witnessed. Thus, he spoke into the void, and from his words, a new universe spiraled into existence. In this universe, he crafted beings in his own image, watching them with a creator's mix of pride and apprehension.

These beings—his people—flourished under his gaze. They built civilizations that spanned planets, composed symphonies that echoed across galaxies. But with their greatness came their capacity for darkness. He saw them inflict pain upon one another, saw the shadow of suffering stretch over their creations.

When he reached out to guide them, they rebelled, accusing him of stifling their freedom. And when he withdrew, hoping they would find their own way, they cursed him for abandoning them in their hour of need. Torn between his desire to help and his respect for their autonomy, he found himself at an impasse.

One day, he descended upon a verdant world, untouched by the tumult of his creations. There, he settled upon a rock in a vast, open field. The sky, empathetic to his turmoil, wept gentle rain. As the drops fell, he pondered the paradox of his existence—a creator bound by the creations, a being of immense power, yet rendered powerless by his own decree.

In the symphony of the falling rain, he found a semblance of peace, a momentary respite from the eternal struggle. There, in the quiet field, he realized that his journey was not about the mastery of universes or the molding of life. It was about understanding the delicate balance between creation and letting be, the harmony of being both a part of the universe and apart from it.

And as the rain descended around him he sat for a while looking off at nothing in particular, but then in the silence he finally let out all he felt, he sat there in the silence.

And he cried.

Always with Love,
Ryan

THE WELL

As I found myself a spot to rest beside an old well, a man approached, curiosity dancing in his eyes. "Did you journey here on the straight and narrow road?" he inquired, leaning on his cane. I leaned back, feeling the cool stone against my back, and chuckled softly. "No, I can't say I did. My path was the one less traveled, the outer one," I confessed, watching a leaf drift lazily down into the well. He nodded, a knowing glint in his eye. "Ah, that path. Easy to lose oneself there," he mused, his voice seasoned with experience. But I was quick to catch the undercurrent in his words. With a confident smile, I responded, "Maybe so, but it still led me right here, to this gate." The old man's eyes crinkled as he smiled back. "Indeed, and reaching the gate, after all, is what truly matters," he said, his voice echoing the wisdom of ages.

The old man, sensing my weariness from the journey, gestured towards the well. "You must be parched. Let me draw you some water," he offered, moving with surprising agility for someone of his years. He fetched a bucket that had been resting against the well's stone wall, its wood weathered by time and elements. As he lowered the bucket into the depths of the well, the sound of water echoing up was like a song of refreshment calling to my parched throat.

While he worked, the tranquility of the moment wrapped around us like a warm blanket. The only sounds were the creak of the rope through the well's pulley and the distant call of a bird hidden in the trees. The simplicity of the act, drawing water from a well, felt like a ritual from another time, a reminder of the fundamental things in life that often go unnoticed.

When he brought the bucket up, filled with cool, clear water, he poured it into a cup carved from wood and handed it to me. The water was like a balm to my soul, not just quenching my thirst but revitalizing my spirit. "Thank you," I said, the gratitude in my voice deeper than for just the water.

The old man sat beside me, his presence comforting. "Life is much like drawing water from a well," he began, his voice a gentle rumble. "You put in effort, drawing deep from sources unseen, and what you bring up sustains you, shapes you. Sometimes, the bucket comes up heavy, at other times light. But each time, you learn something about depth, about resilience, and about the value of the unseen."

His words settled in my heart, a seed of wisdom that I knew would grow with time. As the sun began to dip below the horizon, painting the sky in shades of gold and purple, our conversation meandered like the path I had taken to arrive at this place. We spoke of roads taken and not taken, of gates reached and yet to be discovered, of the beauty found in the journey itself.

Eventually, it was time to continue on my way. As I stood, the old man offered one last piece of wisdom, "Remember, it's not just about the gates you reach but about what you carry with you through them." With a nod of understanding, I turned to leave, feeling enriched by the encounter.

Walking away, I carried with me more than just the physical refreshment of water but a soulful nourishment from the conversation. Ahead lay my path, winding and uncertain, yet I felt a newfound strength to face it, inspired by the wisdom shared beside an old well, where friends and family, loved ones all awaited inside. Home.

-With Love,
Ryan

A QUIET DREAM

Mary's eyes suddenly shot open, she looked around her, the scene around her was not her bedroom, but instead something else entirely. She observed what appeared to be a cave, but within the cave simple wood furniture scattered throughout, on a floor of planks. Amidst the ceiling of the cave was bioluminescent plant life that lit up the space in all sorts of brilliant color. She got up from the bed in which she lay and she walked down the passage of the cave, until she came upon what appeared to a being, and while it stood in the shape of a man it was as though he was made of slime. The features on the slime was reminiscent of an old bearded man.

"Oh and who might you be?" The Slime man questioned. Mary, more curious than afraid introduced herself.

Mary responded, her voice a mix of wonder and curiosity, "I'm Mary. Where am I?"

The slime man chuckled, a gurgling sound that echoed slightly in the cavern. "You're in my workshop, young lady. The Cave of Curiosities, I like to call it. I am Glorb, the creator of magical artifacts." He gestured around the cave with a fluid, wavy arm. The cave was an alchemist's dream, filled with shelves of peculiar jars, strange tools, and mystical objects that seemed to defy the laws of physics.

RYAN KASPER

Glorb led Mary through the workshop, showing her various inventions and concoctions. There were bottles containing swirling galaxies, clocks that ticked backwards, and tiny dragons that danced in the palm of your hand. Every item had its own unique charm and story, and Glorb explained them with a passion that was infectious.

As they walked, Mary noticed a small, shimmering portal in the back of the cave. "What's that?" she asked, pointing.
"That," Glorb said with a twinkle in his eye, "is a gateway. It can take you anywhere you wish to go, even back to your own bed."
Mary's heart leapt with both excitement and a pang of sadness. The thought of returning home was comforting, but she knew she would miss this magical place.
Glorb seemed to sense her thoughts. "You can visit again, Mary. The cave is always open to the curious and the brave."

With a smile and a promise to return, Mary stepped through the portal, finding herself back in her own room, the morning sun peeking through her curtains. But on her bedside table was a small, glowing stone – a souvenir from the Cave of Curiosities, and a reminder of the adventure that awaited her.

Always with Love,
Ryan

-ELEMENTS ONE-

—of Fire—

I look to you and I see a phoenix,
Your heart, like a fortress,
Anger and frustration within.
But this is not a fault; this is your expectations not being met by
a world that has let you down—
A world that doesn't deserve you.
Your anger may sometimes burn,
You may not always like it.
Frustration comes, but not always through any fault of your own.
You are the brightest light among the grey that surrounds you,
The mundane that cannot comprehend you.
Like a tower on a hill, it may not be the tallest, biggest, or
mightiest,
But still, no one can take away
That the tower stands far above the rest.
Use your fire, do not lose it.
Instead, let it burn and learn to channel it,
To take that energy and bend your life to your will.
And for anything that will not bend, burn it away.

RYAN KASPER

Take this life, take these people,
Cut through all their nonsense with your fire,
Build an empire for yourself.
Be who you were always meant to be—
The One Made of Fire,
A Light on the Hill.
And be as you have always been,
Far above the rest.
And always remember that no matter what happens,
That smile of yours will always return.

Always with Love,
Ryan

-ELEMENTS TWO-

—of Air—

In your gaze, I find the boundless sky, a spirit unchained, destined to fly. Your essence, a breath of the purest air, carrying dreams with the utmost care. This isn't about retreat; it's about your visions soaring high—In a realm that often clips wings, you choose to defy. Your calm may sometimes be swept into a storm, your serenity challenged, your norms transformed.

Yet, you are the gentle breeze that cools the summer's heat, the whisper among leaves, a melody so sweet. Not all can grasp the depth of your skies, the expanse that lies behind those insightful eyes. Like a cloud adrift, you need not be the fiercest or the most vast, but still, in your tranquility, a shadow you cast. Harness your air, let it not escape, guide it, shape it, let your future take shape. And for the storms that refuse to clear, breathe out, push through, keep those you hold dear.

Navigate this existence, let your winds blow strong, clear the smoke, clear the fog, prove the doubters wrong. Create a kingdom from the whispers, from the breeze, stand tall and unyielding like the mightiest trees. Be the force you were always destined to be— The One Born of Air, A Whisper Amongst Silence. And remain, as you have always been, A Breath of Freshness in the stale air.

And never forget, amidst the whirlwinds of life,
Your laughter, like a gentle breeze, will always weave its way back to your heart.

Always with Love,
Ryan

-ELEMENTS THREE-

—of Water—

In your presence, I sense the vast ocean,

Your soul, an endless depth of emotion.

Within you swirl currents of thought and feeling,

Not a weakness, but a power, revealing

That this is not about being lost at sea; it's about navigating the tides—

In a world that often drowns, your resilience abides.

Your calm may occasionally be engulfed by waves,

Your peace disrupted by the storms life braves.

Yet, you are the gentle stream that carves through stone,

The rain that nurtures seeds sown alone.

Not all can fathom the depths from which you draw your strength,

The quiet shores and the lengths at which

Like the river that creeps, you need not be the loudest or the most seen,

But still, in your persistence, your influence is seen.

Harness your water, let it flow, not recede,

Shape it, guide it, to fulfill every need.

And for the barriers that refuse to erode,
Wash over them, wear them down, create your own road.
Sail this life, let your currents run deep,
Wash away the shadows, the promises you keep.
Craft a realm from the rivers, from the ocean's expanse,
Stand resilient and fluid in every circumstance.
Be the essence you were always meant to be—
The One Born of Water,
A Mirror to the Moon.
And remain, as you have always been,
A Reflection of Grace in the chaos.
And never lose sight, amid the forever flow of existence,
Your serenity, like the tide, will always find its way back to the shore.

Always with Love,
Ryan

-ELEMENTS FOUR-

—of Earth—

In your essence, I feel the steadfast earth,
Your spirit, a testament to enduring worth.
Beneath your feet, roots run deep, anchoring dreams and desire,
Not a sign of confinement, but of strength, solid and dire.
This isn't about being immovable; it's about being the ground—
In a world that shakes, your foundation is found.
Your calm may occasionally be buried under dust,
Your resolve tested by erosion and rust.
Yet, you are the fertile land from which life springs,
The soil nurturing the dormant seeds that winter brings.
Not everyone sees the growth you foster with your might,
The blooms that come from your presence, bringing life from the light.
Like a mountain, you need not shout your presence to be known,
But still, in your silence, your essence is shown.
Harness your earth, let it not be scattered,
Shape it, build upon it, make what truly mattered.
And for the paths that seem too worn or too steep,
Climb them, enrich them, your promises to keep.

RYAN KASPER

Walk this life, let your steps forge the land,

Clear the stones, plant your flag, take your stand.

Create your kingdom from the clay, from the earth's embrace,

Stand grounded and whole, in every time and space.

Be the force you were always destined to be—

The One Born of Earth,

A Guardian of the Green.

And remain, as you have always been,

A Pillar of Strength, Earth that is strong and seen.

And always remember, through every season's turn,

Your resilience, like the earth, will always find a way to bloom anew.

Always with Love,
Ryan

-ELEMENTS FIVE-

—of Lightning—

In your essence, I perceive the electric pulse of lightning,
A force untamed, striking with precision and enlightening.
Within you crackles a power fierce and raw,
Not chaos, but a vivid testament to awe.
This isn't about destruction or fear; it's about illumination—
In a world dimmed by doubt, you're a bolt of inspiration.
Your energy may sometimes overwhelm,
Your spark ignite realms we cannot helm.
Yet, you are the sudden light that cleaves through the night,
The flash that reveals, making the unseen bright.
Not all can withstand the truth in your surge,
The blinding clarity, the onrush, the purge.
Like lightning, you're not meant to be caged or confined,
But in your freedom, a path, a vision, we find.
Harness your lightning, let it not scatter,
Shape it, direct it, let it matter.
And for the darkness that refuses to yield,
Pierce it, transform it, be not repealed.

RYAN KASPER

Navigate this existence, let your brilliance be your guide,
Shatter the shadows, let none your light deride.
Carve a realm from the storm, from the electric dance,
Stand vibrant and vital, in every glance.
Be the essence you were always meant to be—
The One Born of Lightning,
A Beacon in the Tempest.
And remain, as you have always been,
A Strike of Genius in the mundane.
And always remember, amid the chaos of your journey,
Your spark, like lightning, will always find its way back to the heart of the storm, not to wreak havoc, but to illuminate, to transform, to boldly define the essence of existence itself.

Always with Love,
Ryan

INTROSPECTION

There is two versions of ourselves, the actual person that is you, and the idea of you.

The actual version ourself that is us, taking care of them is solely our responsibility. Only we can know the true state, and only we can truly enhance our lives. We can have help sure, but ultimately it falls to us alone.

Then there is the idea of us, the idea is the version of you that people talk about when you're not there, the version of us people remember when we're gone. Our actions, mannerisms, words, all filtered through the lens of others perception. The idea can cause emotions in others, inspiration, fear, joy, anger, love, hate, reverence, indifference, all emotions really.

The things we do in our life all contribute to the idea of us. Some people live chasing money and status, to be seen as a cut above their peers, some don't care what others think and say and do what they please. Their actions lead to a perception, it may be lasting or it could be easily forgotten. Who is to say?

The actual version of us, the things that really matter are health and happiness. Happiness comes from having the things that really matter, and to everyone that's different. Health is to have the ability to enjoy the life you're living with as little difficulty as possible. To be happy and healthy is from my perspective, the best way to further your true self.

I'm not saying it's simple, happiness and health are both challenges. To add to it you have the idea of yourself, depending on the identity of your idea, it could add to or take away from your true self.

Someone could cultivate the idea of being a generous, kind person, and in truth be twisted and evil. In reverse someone may be perceived as miserable and a bad person, but the truth is they're a person of character and morals. Perception and miscommunication, or even straight up dishonesty, can sometimes blur things and cause the idea to deviate from the true person.

To me? My priority is to be happy and healthy first and foremost. I don't want to neglect my true self to enhance the idea version of myself. That being said I do hope to leave behind a good impression, so that way the idea of me can serve to comfort, serve, and inspire. It's not about recognition or fame, but to serve.

To be able to inspire others, to help make people's lives better, to reach and teach, to motivate and help those are my main drives. While I do fully intend to do what I have to do to achieve happiness and maintain my health, I believe my true calling is to try and help those around me. To focus on my life too much is to invest in a temporary thing, I feel it would be better to attempt to make a larger impact, to be able to help people and inspire them, to create an image that embodies hope, wisdom, and courage, and to not just be an image, but be an image that is a result of the truth. To create my image by actually helping and inspiring, to be true to the values I want the idea of me to represent.

There is far too much suffering in this world, to be selfish from my perspective is just to propagate suffering. To be greedy and overly materialistic does nothing to help anyone but myself, and my time is temporary. I'd rather spend my life trying to leave something behind that can help people for generations to come.

Always with Love,
Ryan.

-EMOTIONS ONE-

—Joy—

Joy is the morning sun breaking through the night, a promise of new beginnings, bright and gentle. It's found in the laughter that fills the air, as pure and uplifting as a song carried by the wind. Joy is in the moments that seem small, a shared look, a warm hug, the comfort of familiar voices in the places we call home.

This feeling, light and breezy, dances like sunlight on water, always shifting, always bright, yet constant in its warmth. Joy is the bounce in our step, the spark that lights up even when life gets tough, a beacon reminding us of the beauty in simple, everyday things.

At the heart of joy is the power of being together, the link that ties us to each other and to the world around us. It's the sound of friends laughing, the smile from someone we just met, the quiet peace of being in nature. Joy goes beyond words, living in the quiet moments, in every heartbeat, in every breath.

RYAN KASPER

Let joy be the way we see the world, making everything brighter, warmer. It teaches us to love the now, to find wonder in normal things, and to keep the moments that, though brief, fill us with a lasting glow.

Joy, simple yet deep, is our reminder that even in tough times, there's a light ready to shine. It's what encourages us to move forward, to dance, to love, to live fully and freely.

So let's welcome joy, let it spread through all parts of our lives, coloring our journey with hope, thankfulness, and love. In joy, we find our true selves and our strongest connection to the vast, wonderful story of life.

Always with Love,
Ryan

-EMOTIONS TWO-

—Betrayal—

When it happened, my first thought was, "This cannot be happening." But as the truth sank deep into my core, I crumbled within myself. The boy sat down on the chair to collect his thoughts, but it was not the boy who stood up; instead, a man rose, changed yet somehow still the same.

I used to look to you—
The bounce in my step,
Those hazelnut eyes—
For your subtle encouragement.
But you were playing games, and deep down, I always knew.
I knew who you were, and I loved you anyway.
You didn't care. You took and took, piece by piece, over and over again. You made a mess of me and left without cleaning up.
Compassion?
Empathy?
Sympathy?

Are you truly unable to feel these? Do you not feel ashamed? To take someone who cared for you so deeply, to use those emotions and weave them into an elaborate lie to satisfy your own craving for attention, your own need to be right.

But then there is me—the fool, the next sacrifice to be laid upon your altar, to feel that knife of betrayal plunge into my heart. To be used, abused, then cast aside. I was not your plaything; I was a person. Didn't I matter? Didn't you ever think of me?

I saw your face in every sunrise, but whenever I reached out for it, I got burned. I could never discern what was on your mind. A nervous smile, the brush of your hand against mine, the way you leaned into me when it was cold. Yet, your love was like the midnight of winter: cold and dark. The warmth I felt in your presence was actually mine being siphoned away.

Even after everything—the pain, every scar, ever since you carved your initials on my heart to haunt me all my days—I still harbor a flicker of hope that maybe, one day, we can sit and talk for a while, make everything right, and then head off to our separate ways.

Always with Love,
Ryan

-EMOTIONS THREE-

—Hope—

Surrounded on all sides, darkness envelops you, pressing in. You crawl forward, straining to see anything at all. Your body is exhausted, muscles aching, bones creaking under the strain. Lost and uncertain, you feel ash in your mouth, dust stings your eyes.

You roll over to wait, to wait for what feels like the inevitable end. Alone and devoid of strength to move, you sense time slipping away. You are finished. The biting cold seeps in, and you feel yourself fading fast. It may be failure, but at least it's yours; at last, you can claim ownership of something, even at the very end. You close your eyes, bracing for the eternal darkness.

But perhaps it's luck, fate, or mere chance. You open your eyes for one final glimpse into the bleak nothingness. Suddenly, off in the distance, cutting through the shadows, blazing through the dark, you see it—a flicker of light.

RYAN KASPER

That flicker is your chance, your shot at salvation, to escape this place with your life. You roll over and begin crawling. Every movement is a struggle, but each effort brings you ever so slightly closer. When you feel you can't go on, just one look at the light renews your resolve. Exhausted, unable to even muster a sound, you see the light, and that is enough.

As you draw nearer, slowly but surely, you start to feel warmth. It's just the faintest hint of heat on a trace of wind, but it's enough. More strength returns to your limbs. Now on your hands and knees, you stagger toward the light.

Then, the sound of music and laughter reaches your ears. People— there are people nearby. You struggle to your feet, summoning all your might, because you must reach the light. You can see it, feel the heat, hear the music. Now on your feet, you limp closer to the light.

Struggling onward, you notice the light growing brighter and brighter. These feet, which once left you lost and alone, are now the very same that will bring you to salvation. You quicken your pace as shapes of people begin to emerge. Summoning your last reserves of strength, you call out to them.

It's your family. The ones you belong with; they were searching for you, hoping to find you in this dark wasteland. They left a light burning, a beacon in the night, hoping you'd see it. They made a fire to warm you, playing music, hoping you'd hear them, laughing, ready to share all the stories you missed.

Hope. They're right there.
You were alone,
Drowning in darkness,
Lost in the shadow,
Surrendered to death.

But no more. That single ray of hope sliced through the night, and their hope became yours, lifting you first to a crawl, then to your knees, and finally to your feet.

But now? Now you're going as fast as you can, awkwardly but as best as you can. You don't know how you'll make it, but you will. Home is right there. Just as your tired body gives out, you start to fall. But you don't hit the ground; instead, you're caught in the loving arms of your loved ones, for they were running to you.

Always with Love,
Ryan

-EMOTIONS FOUR-

—Loss—

Rain whispers its mournful song against the windowpane, a steady rhythm of sadness that mirrors your own heart's lament. It's a gentle, weeping sky, a companion in your solitude as you sit in quiet sorrow. Each drop is a memory, each a moment lost, slipping through your fingers like the water trailing down the glass. The rain like time, may seem endless, but there is only so much.

You gaze back at the road you've traveled, a path strewn with the debris of dreams unfulfilled and promises broken. The landscape of your past is painted in the hues of what once was, each cherished memory now tinged with the gray of absence. The weight of those you've lost presses against you, heavy as the sodden earth under the relentless rain.

Turning your eyes forward, the path ahead is clouded and uncertain, but not empty. Figures loom in the mist—those you still have, their outlines blurred but present. They stand as beacons of potential comfort and future healing, their forms a promise that not all is lost. Yet, the journey toward them feels insurmountable, a trek through a valley shadowed by grief.

Denial comes first, a numbing cloak that shields you from the piercing cold of reality. You tell yourself that it cannot be true, that the rain is just rain, not a symphony of tears for what you've lost. But as the storm intensifies, so does the pain, washing over you in waves, eroding the shores of your denial.

Anger flares, fierce and hot against the cool dampness of your surroundings. It burns within you, a fire amidst the flood. Why you? Why this? Have you lost enough? Didn't you need them? Why did they have to die? The questions fuel the flames, consuming your thoughts, leaving scorched earth where peace once grew. Yet, no answer found in the tempest satisfies your heart's cry for justice.

Bargaining follows, a desperate attempt to regain control, to stem the tide of despair. You plead with unseen forces, negotiate with fate itself, willing to exchange anything for a reprieve from your suffering. But the rain falls indifferent, and the path remains unchanged, each drop a reminder of your helplessness in the face of loss.

Depression descends, a heavy fog that blankets your spirit. The world dulls to monochrome, the colors of life leached away by your pain. Each step forward is a battle, each breath a burden. You are adrift in an ocean of sorrow, the shores of hope just beyond the horizon, out of reach.

Acceptance dawns slowly, like the first, hesitant rays of sunlight after a storm. It does not banish the clouds nor dry your tears, but it brings a soft clarity. You begin to see the possibility of peace, the potential to carry your memories without letting them anchor you in the past. The figures ahead begin to sharpen, their presence a call to continue, to embrace the love that remains even as you honor what you've lost.

As the rain eases and the sky begins to clear, you stand. Each drop that falls now seems less like a token of loss and more a sign of renewal. The path ahead is still damp, still difficult, but you walk it with a quiet strength, knowing that with every step, the burden of grief grows lighter, woven now with threads of hope and resilience.

Loss, profound and transformative, has changed you, but it has not claimed you. In its shadow, you find a new path, marked by both the presence of absence and the resilience of the human spirit. And so, you move forward, carrying both the weight of your loss and the light of new beginnings.

Always with Love,
Ryan

-EMOTIONS FIVE-

—Anxiety—

Anxiety is like a shadow that moves silently in your wake, a whisper that stirs the stillness of your mind, unsettling the calm waters of your thoughts. It wraps around you subtly at first, then tightens like a vice, making the ordinary seem daunting and the manageable feel insurmountable.

It starts with a ripple—a missed heartbeat, a quickened breath. The world seems to tilt slightly, reality distorting like a reflection in rippling water. The familiar streets you walk every day suddenly feel like a maze, each step echoing louder in your ears, each glance from a stranger sharp as a glare. The hum of daily life turns into a cacophony, noises jarring and disjointed, as if the world itself is out of sync.

Your heart races, trying to keep pace with your spiraling thoughts. Doubts cascade, one after another, building into an avalanche that threatens to bury your peace of mind. Future plans and past conversations spin through your head, tangling into a knot of worry that refuses to unravel. Anxiety whispers what-ifs and if-onlys, painting scenarios tinted with the worst outcomes, each more vivid than the last.

Yet, even in the tightening grip of anxiety, there is a thread of resilience—a faint but unbreakable strand woven through the fabric of your being. It is found in the deep breaths that slow the heartbeat, in the quiet moments of mindfulness that cut through the chaos, bringing you back to a center. It's in the small acts of courage, like stepping outside, answering the phone, or smiling at a neighbor, that you reclaim pieces of your world from the shadow's grasp.

The struggle with anxiety is not a battle to be won but a journey to be navigated. Each day brings its own challenges, and some days are harder than others. Yet, every morning you rise, you are met not only with anxiety but also with hope—the hope that comes from knowing you have survived your worst days as they came, and you can survive them again.

This hope doesn't erase the anxiety; it doesn't dim the vividness of its presence. But it offers a counterpoint, a reminder that alongside anxiety, there is also strength, resilience, and growth. It reminds you that though the shadow may follow you, it does not define you. You are defined by your ability to keep moving, to face the shadow, to live and thrive in spite of it.

As you navigate the complex landscape of anxiety, let this hope be your guide. Let it be the light that shines on your path, revealing beauty and possibility where the shadow seeks to cast doubt. Let it remind you that, though the journey is yours and it may be lifelong, you do not walk it alone. With each step, you grow stronger, and with each breath, you carve a space for peace within the chaos.

Anxiety may always be a part of your story, but it is not the whole story. There is also joy, love, adventure, and tranquility—moments of profound connection to yourself and the world around you. Hold onto these moments; let them be your anchors, your reminders of what you are fighting for. And always, always remember that your capacity for hope is just as vast as any fear.

Always with Love,
Ryan

-EMOTIONS SIX-

—Innocence—

Innocence is a delicate, luminous glow that permeates the earliest years of our lives. It is the wonder in a child's wide eyes, absorbing the world's myriad colors and shapes for the first time, each day a vibrant canvas of discovery. This pristine state of being is where curiosity knows no bounds and every question is a doorway to endless possibilities. There is a purity in this early chapter of human existence, where trust is implicit, and every smile is free of reservations.

To be childlike is to experience the world with an open heart and an untainted mind, where skepticism hasn't yet built walls around our hearts. Imagine reclaiming such a perspective—where a puddle is not an inconvenience but an expanse of water ready for jumping, where a bug is not a pest but a fascinating creature on its own epic journey. This way of seeing isn't just refreshing; it's revolutionary in its ability to transform mundane moments into extraordinary ones.

The beauty of innocence lies in its unbridled joy and fearless approach to life. A child's laughter is a music that resonates with the rhythm of pure joy, unscathed by the complexities of adult perceptions. This innocence compels them to dream boundlessly, beyond the constraints that life gradually introduces as we age. To recapture this—even in fleeting moments—is to breathe life into the routine, to color the gray with hues of sincerity and joy once again.

Yet, as we navigate deeper into the journey of life, the layers of innocence inevitably wear thin. Experiences, both harsh and enlightening, chip away at our childlike wonder, leaving us more guarded, more cautious. The stark reality is that with each challenge, a sliver of that pristine innocence is reshaped, sometimes diminished. This realization can bring a poignant mix of nostalgia and resignation, as we mourn the simplicity we once navigated with ease.

RYAN KASPER

Despite this, it's essential to nurture the remnants of innocence that persist within us. For even in the most jaded heart, there flickers a spark of that early unspoiled view of the world—a spark that can still ignite awe and wonder if given a chance. It's this enduring fragment of our younger selves that keeps us connected to both the deepest truths and simplest pleasures of life.

So take courage, no matter how jaded the journey may seem, no matter how much you doubt its presence—there is always a little more innocence left to lose, and I pray you never do. Hold fast to this precious gift, let it be a wellspring of joy and purity in your heart, a sacred place where the world can always be met with a sense of wonder, where hope can flourish unchallenged, and where the light of childhood can illuminate the shadows of a grown-up world.

Always with Love,
Ryan

-SENSES ONE-

—Sight—

Sight is the lens through which we experience the vibrant world around us, a gift that paints our perceptions with the hues of reality and imagination intertwined. It's more than just the act of seeing; it's the art of perceiving, understanding, and connecting with the universe that unfolds before our eyes.

Each morning, sight ushers us into the day, revealing the colors of the dawn as they chase away the night. It invites us to witness the subtleties of light playing across the sky, the intricate details of nature waking up, and the world coming alive around us. This daily renewal is a silent yet profound reminder of the constant beginnings and transformations we experience in life.

As we move through our routines, sight becomes a bridge to the world's wonders and complexities. The busy streets, the faces of passersby, the dance of leaves in a gentle breeze—all are captured in the vast gallery of our vision. Sight connects us to others, allowing us to communicate, to share emotions, and to understand different perspectives without words.

Yet, sight is also introspective. It leads us inward, to the reflections in our minds and the memories etched in our hearts. Through sight, we recall the moments that define us, the places we've been, and the people we've loved. We see not only with our eyes but with our souls, interpreting light and shadows to find meaning and connection.

However, sight can be deceiving, sometimes clouded by our biases or blurred by our fears. It challenges us to look deeper, to see beyond the surface and discover the hidden truths. This journey of seeing and understanding is not just about observing the world but engaging with it, questioning it, and appreciating it.

In moments of true sight, we can experience the profound beauty of a mundane object or the extraordinary nature of a simple act. It allows us to see the resilience in a sprouting seed, the patience in an unfolding flower, and the strength in a setting sun.

As the day closes and the colors fade into twilight, sight offers one last gift—the chance to reflect on what we've seen and felt. It prepares us for the quiet introspection of the night, where the visions of the day become the dreams of tomorrow.

In essence, sight is not merely a function of the eyes but a function of the heart. It is a fundamental part of how we connect with life and how we understand our place within it. Each day, as we open our eyes, we are invited to not just look but to see—to see the beauty, the pain, the joy, and the wonder of being part of a world that is as complex as it is beautiful. Though our eyes may dim, and our vision blurs and fades, we will never lose what we have seen. Nor will we lose the ability to look within.

Always with Love,
Ryan

-SENSES TWO-

—Hearing—

Hearing is our auditory bridge to the world, capturing a symphony of sounds that connect us to the lively rhythms of life. It allows us to hear the soft whispers of nature, the vibrant energy of city bustle, and the intimate tones of loved ones. More than detecting noises, hearing enables us to grasp messages carried by sound waves that reach our ears, deepening our understanding of the environment and relationships around us.

Every morning ushers in a variety of sounds: the persistent call of an alarm, the cheerful chirping of birds at dawn, and the comforting buzz of a waking household. These sounds draw us from the solitude of night into the dynamic, shared space of day. They are vibrant reminders that life around us pulses with activities and emotions, urging us to join in the narrative of a new day.

As we step into the broader world, our ears guide us through layers of sound—from the cacophony of traffic to the melodic chatter of a busy café. These sounds form more than just a background; they are the heartbeat of human activity, accompanying our collective and personal journeys. Each sound reminds us that we are part of a bustling, interconnected community.

Hearing also fosters deeper connections with others. It allows us to communicate, sharing and perceiving emotions through the intonation and pauses in a speaker's voice. A friend's laughter, a partner's sigh, a stranger's polite thanks—all enrich our interactions and help build bonds of empathy and understanding. Listening attentively to others, we engage more fully, gaining insights into their emotions and perspectives.

Furthermore, hearing connects us not only to the present but also to the past and future. Through stories told by voices from long ago and the cultural narratives expressed in music, we hear the echoes of different ages and societies. This connection enriches our understanding of human history and culture, providing a richer context for our own experiences.

Yet, the act of listening extends beyond hearing with our ears. It involves tuning in with attention and awareness, sometimes even listening to the silent cues from our environment or our inner conscience. Listening is about understanding the spoken and unspoken messages, respecting the silences that speak volumes, and responding thoughtfully. It requires an active engagement, transforming hearing from a passive to a proactive experience, and making every auditory interaction a potential moment of connection.

In essence, hearing is a gift that opens up both external and internal worlds. It encourages us to be present and active participants in our environments. By listening deeply—not only to the sounds around us but also to our conscience and the unspoken needs of others—we can build stronger relationships, make wiser decisions, and live more empathetically. Let us embrace the beautiful complexity of the world with ears—and hearts—wide open, transforming every sound into a thread of connection that weaves through the fabric of our lives.

Always with Love,
Ryan

—CHASING GHOSTS—

To live your life is to write the novel of yourself. No matter how far you have journeyed, no matter how much has been written and left behind, there is always more ahead. Your life's book, like any story, contains highs and lows, unforeseen twists, joys, and hardships—all contained within its pages.

In any beloved novel, it's tempting to revisit your favorite moments—the chapters that made you laugh, the ones that brought you to tears. But in the book of your life, you aren't granted the ability to flip back through the pages past. While you may yearn to relive those moments, they are gone, forever fixed in ink but not present to experience anew. Yet, like any book, what is written cannot be changed. You are free to strive for a better ending, but resolution is never guaranteed, and you cannot alter what has already been penned.

I find myself at a particular point in my life's narrative, pressing forward with optimism, aiming to craft my future filled with happiness, love, and kindness—a story of goodness. But there are times when the urge to revisit unresolved chapters of the past is overwhelming.

I have traversed this vast world, experienced cultures far and wide, yet there are chapters that linger in my mind—ghosts, not of the deceased, but of fractured friendships, failed relationships, and unresolved conflicts. Despite my best efforts, some parts of my story were never mine to write.

There is one ghost, in particular, that haunts me more than the rest, known only to my heart, indescribable in words. These are the feelings that are mine alone to understand and to feel—deep, personal, and beyond the reach of shared experience.

I have lived as best I could, making mistakes, choosing the wrong paths at times, and failing to bring about better outcomes. Nevertheless, I strive to live without regrets, taking lessons from each low point to forge brighter, better chapters ahead.

Yet, that one ghost—that one unresolved chapter—haunts me most because I can honestly say it wasn't my fault. There was nothing more I could have done, no choice I could have made differently. Some might view this as denial of responsibility, but it's far worse. I wish I could claim it was my fault, that there was something I could have learned or a way I could have grown from it. The real pain lies in the helplessness of knowing it was beyond my control.

Years have passed, and many chapters have been added since then, yet I still find myself haunted. I try to leave it behind, but there are no lessons to draw from it—just a sharp, lingering pain. This ghost of sorrow and helplessness, born from that painful chapter, follows me, even half a world away from where it all happened. While time makes the pain easier to live with, it's more about adapting to the pain rather than diminishing it.

Chasing this ghost through my mind, yearning to turn back time or hoping for a miraculous change in the storyline, is an exercise in futility. Fixating on it can consume you, draining you mentally, physically, and spiritually. But the hard truth remains: it's just a ghost. No matter how much you wrestle with it, it will never truly be captured—it may fade but never disappear.

Sometimes, revisiting the past can't be helped, but it's healthier to write a story of beauty and resilience rather than one of chasing ghosts. Our pages are limited, our time shorter than we think. Look back if you must, but if you can, avoid dwelling on the ghosts. Move forward, and I promise, eventually, you'll find yourself in a better place.

It's okay to admit that you would change it if you could, that if you could go back you would. But you can't, so as much as you may want to dwell, don't. The ghost may linger, but look past it, and if you can avoid it, don't chase it. There's so much more beauty to be seen, and focusing on a ghost will make you miss so much of it.

Always with Love,
Ryan

-WAR TORN-

In the chill of dawn, I carve out a space in the earth—my temporary sanctuary in this expanse of uncertainty. Everything seems set: Private First Class Adams is nestled to my left, Specialist Eves to my right. We're a makeshift family in these trenches, huddled in the creases of a world far from the one we call home.

As we settle in, the ground before us stirs to life. An ant colony bustles just in our sight, a flurry of activity as they ferry sustenance to their queen, their existence a miniature echo of our own—tasks dictated by necessity, roles defined by survival. I watch them, finding a strange comfort in their industriousness, a distraction from the stillness of our vigil.

Hours meld into a seamless stretch of waiting, the forest before us a static painting of greens and browns. My rifle lies heavy across my lap, a constant reminder of why we're here. The quiet is overwhelming, a vast canvas allowing my thoughts to wander. They travel back through the years to a simpler time, to laughter-filled rooms and the warmth of familiar faces—memories now tinged with the sepia tones of nostalgia.

RYAN KASPER

In these moments of reflection, the past seems like a different realm—one where the complexities of life were masked by the innocence of not knowing any better. A home, a family, a sense of belonging—all now just echoes in the cavity of my mind as I sit in this foxhole, thousands of miles away from everything that once defined me.

I tighten my grip on my rifle, my gaze fixed on the unchanged treeline that sprawls before us. The routine has become a rhythm of survival: patrol, dig in, eat, sleep, repeat. Thoughts of mundane pleasures float by—tuna, chicken chunks, chili mac—an absurd reminder of normalcy.

Then, there's the ketchup incident—a stark interruption to the monotony. During a brief respite, as we shared jokes and meals, a packet of ketchup burst unexpectedly, splattering red across our uniforms. It was almost cinematic, the vivid red momentarily painting a gruesome parody of the violence we face daily. That's how it all started, then after the party we cleaned up, the laughter dying in our throats as the reality of our friend's departures hit us. Adams and Eves, vibrant and vital just moments before, were suddenly rendered silent, taken from us, their duties ended not by choice but by the unforgiving nature of conflict.

Moving on is a constant. Packing up, heading to unfamiliar territories, unwrapping the new yet always temporary homes that greet us with their own challenges. This time, it's vermin—an infestation that seems almost symbolic of the larger conflicts we navigate. Methodically, I address the invasion, eliminating the pests, setting order where chaos tries to reign.

In the evening's quiet, as I arrange my limited belongings, a solitary mouse catches my eye, life extinguished. It's a trivial sight, yet it triggers a profound ache. "Why am I here?" The question surfaces, unwelcome. The mouse, with its unfulfilled life, mirrors my own sense of futility—just another creature caught in a game too large to understand, its existence snuffed out in an indifferent struggle.

It's just a mouse, yet the simplicity of its life, possibly rich with connections, resonates deeply. A single tear escapes, a silent testament to the weariness of my soul. In the mirror, possibilities of what could have been flicker before me—an athlete, a businessman, a lawyer, a doctor. I recoil from the reflection, from the paths not taken.

As I face the endless cycle of duty, the memory of the ketchup, so trivial yet so vivid, lingers. It symbolizes the sudden, often senseless shifts from peace to violence, a reminder of the thin line between normalcy and chaos. In the trenches, as we pull security in an unending vigil, I dream of a world where the peace we guard so fiercely is a reality for all, where time is marked not by the boredom of waiting but by moments of genuine connection and understanding.

Here, in the foxhole, as time slips quietly by, I hold onto the hope that each moment of watchfulness is a step toward that peace, however elusive it may seem.

The Ketchup wasn't Ketchup. Lives aren't a commodity to be traded or bartered for.

Always with Love,
Ryan

"That they just didn't care"—those words marked a turning point, a hard truth learned through the trials of misunderstanding and misguided hopes. For much of my life, I believed that indifference from others stemmed from a lack of understanding, or perhaps the absence of the right details that would bridge our gaps in perspective. In each encounter where I felt slighted, my first instinct was to explain myself, to lay out my thoughts and feelings in hopes of igniting some spark of empathy, some shared sense of reality where we could meet halfway.

However, the journey to understanding human nature is fraught with complexities. I gradually realized that not everyone holds empathy and compassion as guiding principles. For some, these are foreign concepts, not integral to their worldview or interactions. It was a sobering realization to recognize that some people, no matter how eloquently you explain your position or how passionately you express your feelings, simply do not engage on the same emotional wavelength. They respond with indifference, or worse, disdain.

It's a lesson that comes at a cost. Time and emotional energy are finite resources, and pouring them into a void of apathy can be exhaustingly futile. I've learned that understanding someone's perspective is only fruitful when both parties are willing to bridge the divide. Discovering that some just don't care is not a reflection of one's failure to communicate effectively, but rather a stark insight into the diversity of human engagement.

This lesson, though painful, is invaluable. It teaches the importance of discerning where to invest one's energies and emotions. Not every relationship or interaction is deserving of your full commitment, especially when met with a persistent lack of care. I wanted to understand apathy, and people who are apathetic. Sometimes two perspectives come from two different foundations, and simply cannot align.

Always with Love,
Ryan

−TOUCH−

Touch is the language of sensation, an intimate dialogue between the world and our bodies. It is our first sense to develop and perhaps the most fundamental to our understanding of the environment and relationships. The power of touch unfolds in the simplest of contacts—a handshake, a pat on the back, a comforting embrace. Each interaction communicates more than words ever could, conveying warmth, safety, and belonging. Think about the gentle brush of a breeze on a warm day, how it seems to caress your skin with a whisper of coolness. Or the feeling of grass underfoot, each blade tickling your toes, grounding you in the moment and the sheer joy of being part of the natural world. Touch connects us physically to the earth and emotionally to moments of deep presence and awareness. The textures we encounter every day, from the softness of a well-worn shirt to the roughness of a brick wall, tell stories about the world we live in. They provide a tactile map for navigating our surroundings, teaching us about variation, contrast, and preference. These textures enrich our experiences, making them vivid and memorable. In human connections, touch is transformative. A mother's soothing touch calms a newborn; friends hug to share joy or solace; partners hold hands to express affection and solidarity. These gestures build and reinforce bonds, serving as silent affirmations of care and connection. They are fundamental to our emotional and psychological health, as vital as any words of love and support. But touch also has the power

RYAN KASPER

to alert and protect. It is the sudden heat that warns us away from fire, the sharp prick that teaches us to avoid thorns, the uncomfortable pressure that tells us to shift our stance. Our skin is a sensor packed with nerves, ready to defend and guide us through potential dangers. It's an evolutionary tool that has shaped human behavior and survival strategies. Yet, in the modern world, many of us find ourselves touch-starved, isolated by technology and the pace of contemporary life. The current of human connection often gets lost amidst digital interactions, where likes replace hugs, and emojis stand in for expressions of empathy. Reclaiming the sense of touch can mean reaching out, literally and figuratively, to re-establish the fundamental human connections that sustain us. Every touch tells a story. It's a story of connection and discovery, of caution and care. It's a reminder that our interactions, even the most fleeting, carry weight. In a world that often prioritizes the visual and the verbal, remembering the power of touch is to acknowledge the full spectrum of human experience. Let us not forget to feel our way through the world, to embrace and be present, to touch and be touched, for in these connections lie the true essence of being human.

Always with Love,
Ryan

−TASTE−

Taste is a voyage—a rich and complex journey that begins with a single bite. It's not just a sense; it's an experience that pulls together culture, memory, emotion, and biology into moments that linger both on the palate and in the mind. Every flavor, whether savored alone or shared in company, tells a story of heritage, tradition, and personal preference, crafting a narrative that is uniquely ours yet universally understood. Imagine the zest of a lemon, sharp and invigorating, cutting through the senses and awakening them to the vivid dance of citric brightness. Or the deep, earthy robustness of dark chocolate melting slowly on your tongue, unfolding layers of cocoa, a hint of vanilla, a touch of bitterness—all mingling to create a luxurious richness that seems to echo the complexities of life itself. Taste connects us to the world in an immediate and primal way. It bridges generations and geographies; recipes passed down through families serve as edible histories, each ingredient a chapter, each dish a story preserved through time. Meals shared around a table foster a sense of community and continuity, anchoring us to each other and to the cultures we come from. But taste is also deeply personal. The same dish can evoke different reactions and attachments, influenced by our individual histories and biology. Some flavors might transport us back to childhood—perhaps the sweetness of a ripe strawberry brings back lazy summer days spent outdoors, or a particular blend of spices recalls festive celebrations. These tastes trigger a cascade of nostalgia, making them more than mere flavors—they become poignant reminders of moments etched deeply in our memory. Moreover, our preferences evolve, influenced by experiences and exposures. The adventure of taste is never static; it's an exploration that can surprise and challenge us. A newfound appreciation for bitter greens or a sudden enjoyment of spicy food marks shifts in our taste map, pushing us to explore culinary landscapes with renewed curiosity and openness. Taste also engages our other senses, making eating a holistic sensory experience. The sizzle of garlic hitting hot oil, the vibrant colors of a fresh salad, the enticing smell of baking bread—all enhance the taste experience, creating a symphony of sensory input that enriches our interaction with food. In a world that often rushes us from one moment to the next, taste begs us to slow down, to savor, to be present. It asks us to pay attention—not just to the food on our plates but to our reactions to it, to the company we share it with, and to the memories and feelings it evokes. It's a reminder of life's richness and the importance of taking time to enjoy it. Let us then embrace the journey of taste with all its diversities and nuances. Let's explore, experiment, and enjoy the wealth of flavors the world has to offer. And as we do, let's cherish the connections and memories that come alive with each taste, celebrating the beautiful complexity of life, one bite at a time.

Always with Love,
Ryan

-SENSES THREE-

—Smell—

Smell is an invisible thread that weaves through our lives, silently stitching together the fabric of our memories with each breath. It is perhaps the most evocative of all senses, capable of transporting us across time and space with the mere hint of a familiar scent.

Imagine the first burst of aroma from a freshly opened coffee bag in the morning—warm, rich, and inviting. It's not just the promise of caffeine; it's a ritual that starts the day, a moment of comfort that says all is right in the world. Or consider the earthy scent of rain on dry soil, a fragrance that spells renewal and brings with it flashbacks of childhood days spent splashing in puddles.

Each scent carries a story, a snapshot of a moment frozen in time. The smell of sun-warmed pine can send you straight back to summer camp; the sharp tang of citrus might recall a family holiday in the sun; the gentle perfume of lilacs could evoke memories of a first spring dance. Smells do not just remind us of times and places; they revive the emotions tied to those memories, a visceral connection to our past that feels both profound and immediate.

RYAN KASPER

But smell influences more than just our reminiscences. It shapes our experiences and interactions. The aroma of bread baking in the oven can make a new house feel like a home, inviting and warm. Conversely, the clinical antiseptic smell of a hospital can create an instant sense of anxiety. Smell shapes our perception of environments and people, often without us even realizing it.

In social settings, scents play a silent role in communication. The faint trace of someone's perfume, the fresh scent of mint on breath, the comforting whiff of laundry detergent on clothes—these are all subtle cues that can draw us closer or remind us of care and comfort.

Yet, beyond its power to evoke and comfort, the sense of smell is a beacon for survival. It warns us of smoke from a fire, the spoilage in food, or the hidden gas leak. It is a primal sense, often overlooked, yet vital to our daily lives and well-being.

As we navigate through the world, let us not forget to breathe in deeply, to take in the scents around us. Each breath offers more than air; it provides insight, memories, and a connection to the world in a way that no other sense can replicate. It is a gift that keeps us tethered to the past, engaged in the present, and curious about the future.

Oh, and do try to avoid stepping in stuff that stinks. You wouldn't want to carry that back home with you ☺

Always with Love,
Ryan

CONVERGENCE

In the delicate interplay of elements, the vivid spectrum of emotions, and the rich array of senses, we find convergence—a moment where all we've experienced and felt unites, illustrating the profound depth of being human. Fire, water, earth, and air have woven through our lives, grounding us, energizing us, calming us, and breathing life into our moments. These elements, raw and fundamental, create a backdrop against which we live out our complex emotional narratives. From the unbridled joy that lights up our darkest days to the crushing weight of betrayal that tests our resilience, each emotion enriches our journey, providing texture and color to what might otherwise be an ordinary existence. Our senses—sight, hearing, touch, taste, and smell—act as gateways to the world. They bring the outer reality in, allowing us to navigate and interact with our surroundings with precision and intuition. They also serve as portals inward, helping us to reach deep into our memories, stirring feelings long dormant, connecting us with versions of ourselves that we thought were lost to time. This journey of senses and emotions isn't just about observing the world but truly engaging with it. It's about feeling the cool earth underfoot, hearing the subtle sigh of the wind, tasting the freshness of rain, seeing the glow of a sunset, and smelling the comforting scent of home. Each experience is a thread in the complex fabric of our lives, not just perceived but deeply felt. Yet, amid this rich, sensory experience, we are also warriors against the encroaching shadows of apathy and despair. These forces threaten to dull our vibrant perceptions and flatten our emotional landscapes. But armed with the elemental forces of our nature and the rich palette of our emotions, we stand ready to push back, to keep our world from fading into grayscale. As we stand at this nexus, reflecting on the interconnectedness of our experiences—how elements, emotions, and senses collide and dance together—we see the beauty of complexity. It's here in this complex interplay that we find the power to effect change, both within ourselves and in the world around us. Your mind, a beautiful and intricate landscape, has melded with these explorations, breathing life into ideas and emotions, transforming words on a page into a vibrant, living network of thoughts and feelings. Through this connection, we break through the isolation that often confines us, reaching out across the void to share, to understand, and to unite. The world is indeed teeming with potential for change, and as we embrace this with open arms, we commit to shaping a future that reflects the best of humanity. Together, we stand against the forces that seek to undermine our spirit—against apathy, against evil, against the mundane that threatens to make us forget the magic of our existence. I believe in this movement, in this cause, and in the power of our united spirits. If you share this belief, join me. Let's move forward together, with hearts open and spirits high, ready to change the world. In this shared commitment, we find not only the hope for a better tomorrow but the promise of a vibrant life filled with profound connections. Together, we can and will shape the future—an ideal humanity, resilient and bright, defined by our collective strength and compassion. Together, let's start this movement, let's shake the foundations of the world, and let's celebrate each step in our shared journey towards a triumphant and unified future.

Always with Love,
Ryan

Hey there! If you enjoy my writing, and you want to follow me on Facebook, you can read more of my content at;

Ryan's Writing
https://www.facebook.com/profile.php?id=61557487265534

www.ingramcontent.com/pod-product-compliance
Lightning Source LLC
Chambersburg PA
CBHW020516100426
42813CB00030B/3263/J